CYBERSENSE

THE LEADER'S GUIDE TO PROTECTING CRITICAL INFORMATION

ACTION GUIDE

By

Prof. Derek Smith

"The Worlds #1 Cybersecurity Expert"

Speaker, Author, Writer, Educator

National Cybersecurity Education Center Publishing

Bowie, MD

HELP OTHERS TO PROTECT THEIR CRITICAL INFORMATION!

"Share This Book"

Retail for $19.97

Quantity discounts are available!

To place an order contact:

info@NCSEConline.com

THE IDEAL PROFESSIONAL SPEAKER FOR YOUR NEXT EVENT

Any organization that wants to develop their people's knowledge of cybersecurity needs to hire Derek for a keynote and/or workshop training!

TO CONTACT OR BOOK DEREK TO SPEAK OR TRAIN:

National Cybersecurity Education Center

www.ncseconline.com

301 744-7355

derek@ncseonline.com

or

derekasmith.com

derek@derekasmith.com

First Edition

ISBN-13: 978-1979600842

Table of Contents

Introduction

Today, any leader who is not concerned about the cybersecurity of their business or organization is simply neglecting their due diligence in protecting the organization. Prudence demands that cybersecurity is essential for every forward-thinking leader. Cybersecurity is no longer optional for *any* organization, and leaders must usher in and understand advance cybersecurity to prevent data compromise.

The costly problem of data breaches is not going away anytime soon. Stolen data equals big money for cybercriminals. Any information and technologies asset that provides rewards/money with minimum effort is vulnerable. In fact, The Identity Theft Resource Center says that, according to their mid-year report, "The number of U.S. data breaches tracked through June 30, 2017, hit a half-year record high of 791 (Identity Theft Resource Center 2017). The ITRC says they anticipate the number of breaches could reach 1,500 in 2017, which would be a 37 percent annual increase over 2016.

Cybercriminals are not just passing through. They are setting up camp and improving their technologies. Leaders must do the same. They no longer have the option of hiding behind fear of technology and the lack of understanding of cybersecurity. Procrastination and thinking that *someday* you'll get around to taking a course and learning what must be done to protect your business has been the devastating mistake that many leaders have made to the demise of their business.

Today is the day to get the education you need regarding cybersecurity, and this book is the start of understanding the benefits and implementation of cybersecurity for your business. Every day that you put off the responsibility of cybersecurity is another day that your organization is vulnerable.

Cybersense—The Leader's Guide to Protecting Critical Information is a comprehensive guide written by Derek Smith, the Worlds #1 Cybersecurity Expert, that contains critical and practical information for helping leaders devise strategies to protect their company from data compromise. This guide answers the following questions and many others for which all leaders need answers:

- Exactly what is cybersecurity?
- Why is cybersecurity important to my organization?
- Is my business a good candidate for cybersecurity measures?
- How can I protect my organization from data compromise?
- How can I continually monitor the security of my organization's data with constant cyber threats occurring?
- How can I implement cybersecurity quickly and efficiently?

Leaders do not leave any other critical systems in their organization vulnerable to attack. Why would they leave information assets and technologies vulnerable when there is a simple solution to the vulnerability? Fear of the unknown may contribute to the hesitation to move forward with cybersecurity. It is important to note that cybersecurity has now become the responsibility of leaders. It is no longer reserved for the behind-the-scenes techies and geeks. Leaders need a firm understanding of how they can best protect their organization whether they are the Chief Information Security Officer for the organization or are required to work closely with the CISO. Effective leaders must be proactive to learn what they need to know.

This ACTION PLAN, written by a trusted industry leader, is a companion workbook for the book *Cybersense: The Leader's Guide to Protecting Critical Information*. The ACTION PLAN serves as a resource for evaluating your company's cybersecurity situation and helping you make quality decisions. The workbook also emphasizes key information from the book to serve as a quick reference guide.

1: Why Leaders Must Take Cybersecurity Seriously

ACTION: Take cybersecurity in your organization seriously!

There are several reasons that leaders must take cybersecurity seriously. In Chapter 1, you read about some of the reasons:

- ✓ Cybercriminals are hyper-vigilant in their work to stay one step ahead of business leaders.
- ✓ Cybercriminals value your company's assets for their own use, including your confidential data and critical information.
- ✓ Cybercriminals use the latest technology to do their work.
- ✓ Cybercriminals attack businesses of all sizes and find a sweet spot for attacks on small businesses.
- ✓ Cybercriminals can do extensive harm to a business financially, reputation/branding, and the loss of valuable employees and loyal customers.
- ✓ Organizations can be held liable, in some instances, to customer information that is compromised in a cyberattack.
- ✓ A major cyberattack may give your competitors an advantage in the marketplace.

Take Action in Your Organization

1. Do YOU take cybersecurity seriously?

2. On a scale of one to ten, how vigilant are you to stay one step ahead of the cybercriminals that can target your business?

3. What critical information and confidential data does your business hold and store on computers and online (such as in the Cloud) that would be valuable to cybercriminals? (Make a general list.)

4. On a scale of one to ten, if this information were to be stolen, how severely would it impact your business?

5. Is it a priority for your business to purchase and use current technology for the business? Why or why not?

6. Have you received legal advice regarding liability in the event of a cyberattack? In what ways would your organization be liable if it suffered a cyberattack?

7. Do you believe your business is vulnerable to a cyberattack? Why or why not?

8. Do you believe that cybersecurity is something that should be left to the IT department or that you, the business leader (owner, manager) should be involved? Why or why not?

9. If your business suffered a cyberattack that shut down operations for even a few days, which of your competitors would have an automatic advantage in the marketplace because of the shutdown?

10. Which competitors would be most likely to instantly pounce on the opportunity to take this advantage?

11. Would your business survive another six months if a strong competitor was able to take advantage of your loss due to a cyberattack?

2: Cybercriminals and Cybercrime

ACTION: Understand cybercriminals and cybercrime so you can protect your organization

In Chapter 2, you learned that cybercriminals are not always whom they seem to be. Cybercriminals don't necessarily hide away in dark basements. They may be your neighbor, local retailer, server at your favorite restaurant, or even an employee in your business. The important thing to understand is that *anyone* with which you communicate, do business, or share files/information could be a cybercriminal and steal your data or information.

You know that some of the major players in cybercrime are the following:

✓ Hackers
✓ Hacktivists
✓ Employees
✓ Industry Competitors
✓ Financial gainers

Take Action in Your Organization

1. Of the five main types of cybercriminals listed above, which are the most likely to target *your* business? Why?

2. What makes you most vulnerable to the cybercriminals that you listed as the most likely to target your business?

3. What specific action will you take against this specific type of cybercriminal now that you've identified it?

4. Cybercrime can be divided into two main categories:

- Crimes that use computer networks to carry out other criminal activities such as phishing, fraud, identity theft, and cyberstalking
- Crimes that directly target computer networks or devices such as cell phones with viruses and denial-of-service attacks, rendering the computer or device locked or useless.

Does your business provide employees with laptops and cell phones for business use? Which departments/ employees are provided company laptops and/or cell phones?

5. Are your employees allowed to use their work laptops and cell phones for personal use also or only business? If so, what concerns do you have regarding personal use of company devices?

6. What kind of training has been provided for your employees regarding the emails they have permission to receive/send on their business laptops or cell phones?

7. Do you and your employees understand the following types of attacks? Write the definition of each type of attack:

   - Phishing

   - Fraud

   - Identity theft

   - Cyberstalking

   - Denial of Service

   - Viruses

8. What policies and procedures are currently in place for each type of attack listed above?

9. Are the current policies effective? If so, why? If not, why not?

3: Cybersecurity Knowledge Is the Leader's Responsibility

ACTION: Take responsibility for your education regarding cybersecurity.

Cybercriminals are productive and knowledgeable enough about technology to constantly roll out new types of attacks, particularly against companies that leave open doors for cybercriminals to enter the business, including small businesses and huge corporations. It's apparent that no business can afford to ignore cybersecurity without creating tremendous risk and possibly the failure of the company to thrive or survive.

But it's not all bad news on the cybersecurity front. A capable leader can mitigate the risks and effects of malicious cyber activity by implementing preventive measures, detecting malicious activity, and responding to the activity in a timely and effective manner.

Take Action in Your Organization

1. As a leader in your organization, do you recognize the responsibility you have for understanding cybersecurity for your organization? Please explain.

2. What actions show that you take your responsibility for cybersecurity seriously? Explain.

3. Do you leave all cybersecurity issues with the IT department of your company? Explain why or why not?

4. What security decisions must you make as a leader of your organization?

5. What is the mindset of a leader who takes cybersecurity seriously?

6. Expound on each task/concept of the cybersecurity-savvy leader based on the graphic below.

4: Cybersecurity—An Underlying Issue

ACTION: Understand the underlying issues with cybersecurity so you can create a firm foundation for further effective steps to protect your business.

Once you and your staff understand the underlying issues and implement these three preventive principles, you will see an immediate improvement in cybersecurity in your organization. Understanding the underlying issues can also create momentum for launching your cybersecurity strategy details.

1. Label each of the three triangle sides with one of the three underlying issues of cybersecurity.

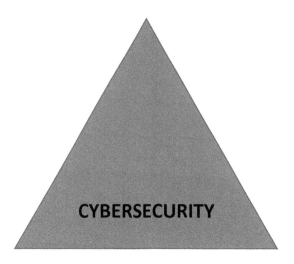

2. Does your company use a two-authentication system, such as requiring both a username and password, for all confidential or sensitive information? Why or why not?

3. Taking measures with confidentiality helps prevent important sensitive information from reaching the wrong people while making sure it reaches the intended recipient that is allowed access to the information. For the enforcement of confidentiality, information that is confidential should be categorized as such, and only those who are authorized to view the confidential information should have access to it. Determining who should have access to confidential material stored online or sent back and forth via email and the level of confidentiality of the information should be predetermined.

   How tight is the **confidentiality** security at your company? Rate these confidentiality issues from one to five with one being the least secure and five being highly secure. For each issue, tell why you gave it the rating you did.

- ✓ Password and username required for logging on to computers _____

- ✓ Password and username required to access cell phone _____

- ✓ Password and username required to access confidential files/information _____

- ✓ Password and username required to access bookkeeping software/apps _____

- ✓ Password and username required to access financial records _____

- ✓ Security code and identification required to enter building or room where confidential paper files are stored _____

4. **Integrity** is all about ensuring that data remains accurate consistently throughout its life cycle. It is critical that the company can trust that the data is accurate and original and has not been modified. Data integrity security includes implementing security practices that help protect the data from being compromised by being modified or deleted by parties with malicious intent or without authorization to do so.

Does your company take security measures to ensure the integrity of data from outsiders? If so, what security measures are taken? Explain.

Does your company take security measures to ensure the integrity of data from internal people? If so, how?

5. What are the criteria used by your company to determine which employees are authorized to access and modify confidential or sensitive data? Explain.

6. Businesses are hosts to various forms of confidential information, *not just customer information,* that thieves may steal for their malicious benefit. List some other types of confidential information/data that thieves might consider to be of value. Circle the types of information/data that could be at risk at your company.

7. Besides computer files, where else can cybercriminals steal information/data from your company?

8. Fill in the blanks in the following sentences:

   In this rapidly evolving environment where networks are increasing in size and capacity, the focus must be on _____ and _____ the risks associated with cyber threats.

   _____ is the best course of action for any company when it comes to data theft.

Take Action in Your Organization

List the employees (and their department) that are authorized to access and modify confidential and sensitive data. Tell why each has access. Don't forget to list people for outsourced jobs.

Name	Department or Job	Reason for Access

5: How Cybersecurity Works

ACTION: Study the ten dimensions of cybersecurity and make sure you understand them, so you can be effective in taking responsibility for cybersecurity in your organization.

The ten dimensions of cybersecurity is a *framework* that you can use for managing cybersecurity performance. It is a roadmap, of sorts, that can help you focus on safeguarding crucial data from critical threats.

1. Become familiar with **the ten dimensions of cybersecurity** as shown in the graphic on the next page. List the ten dimensions of cybersecurity here:

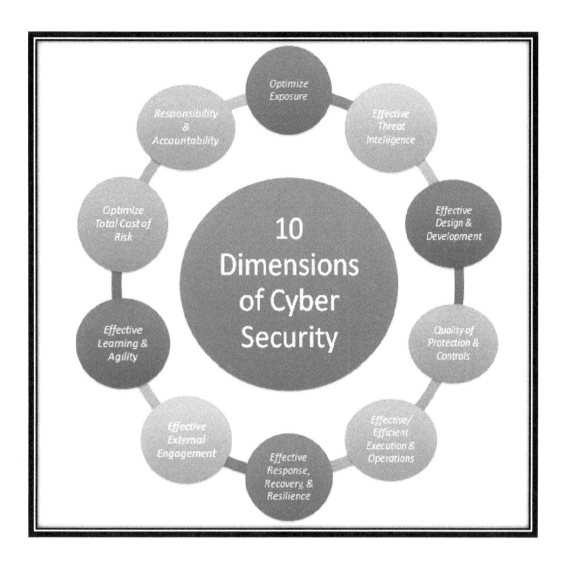

In the realm of cybersecurity, people interact with a *system*. Through those interactions, certain events or instances may arise that may have a positive or negative effect on your business. The people who interact with the system may be a part of the business, or they may be external parties. They could be individuals or an organization other than your organization, interacting with a device, computer, or software through which an event may or may not arise. The systems these people interact with could be a technology, information, process, or a combination of these things, along with the physical facilities that enable the people to interact with the systems. These people must also have access to certain types of support-providing facilities that are physical in nature to facilitate the interaction process.

2. In your organization, do you have external parties that interact with your data system? Explain.

3. List the generic (not specific names) external parties that generally interact with your data system.

4. To what extent do these external parties interact with your system? And how do they interact? Explain.

5. Not only must you focus on minimizing the threats and risk associated with information sharing through good cybersecurity practices, but you must also understand how to strengthen the security measures that are already in place for the business.

   In your opinion, how effective are the cybersecurity protocols at your company? Explain your answer.

6. List the three important factors that should be considered when employing the cybersecurity practices within your organization.

6: Dimension One—Exposure Optimization

ACTION: Understand how user access and exposure affects your system and how you can optimize the system for access without high risks.

You have users and systems that interact with one another, and their interaction leads to events. Optimizing exposure is the starting point for the performance of all cybersecurity measures in place within your business. You must understand and optimize the exposure of information and systems to breaches, attacks, or violations.

Exposure mediates between actors and systems. Exposure means that the users have access to the system and all systems are visible. Hence, the systems may be potentially vulnerable. Optimization means balancing tradeoffs, i.e., the negative interactions (in which a system's breach occurred) and positive interactions (in which only the authorized party gained access to the system).

1. As a manager, do you understand when and where to expose parties to critical/confidential/sensitive information? Explain.

2. As a manager do you have criteria and a process in place for monitoring the number of people in your organization that can view specific pieces of information to prevent impromptu and unintentional cyberthreats? If so, what are your criteria and process? Explain.

3. The exposure optimization dimension is based on which two components?

4. The intelligence component involves observing the level of cybersecurity protection your business currently possesses and then evaluating this current standard. Then you must decide where your current cybersecurity efforts stand, compare this against the changing environment, and decide the desired protection level to obtain maximum security against malicious cyber activity. This process is known as performing a *gap analysis.*

   Along with the gap analysis, the intelligence component must also answer certain key questions that will help you obtain a clear picture of where your cybersecurity level currently stands. Answer these questions to help you determine whether there are any flaws in your cybersecurity policies and, if there are, what can be done to close the gaps:

- What information is exposed?

- What information is not exposed?

- What information should be exposed?

- What information should not be exposed?

- Are we currently meeting the standard for what should be exposed?

- Are we currently exposing information that should not be exposed? What should we do about it?

- What action plan and strategies can help us attain the maximum level of cybersecurity?

5. **Execution** includes implementing some of the common security practices and general policies related to cybersecurity such as access, control, system configurations, remediation, privileges, vulnerability detection, and related policies. The execution component is not only the technical aspects of cybersecurity but also involves the Human Resources department to create policies that regulate information disclosures and the penalties associated with the disclosure of information.

Does your organization work with the HR department help define privacy, proprietary, and confidentiality of information penalties? If not, what guidance do you use for creating policies to regulate information disclosures and the penalties associated with the disclosure of information? Explain.

6. You must determine how well your cybersecurity practices are working in the dimension of optimized exposure. Evaluate your company by answering the following questions. (Ask your IT department for assistance if you don't know the answers.)

   - How well are we currently performing in preventing our information systems exposure?

   - How much do we know about the exposure of information within the system and the cyber threats faced by the organization?

- Are we aware of any blind spots in the system? If we are, then what are we doing to offset the effects and bridge the gaps emerging within the system?

- Have we made any discoveries in the significant exposure areas? Are we addressing the areas and increasing security?

- How well have we fared in executing the decisions we have made so far?

- What is the evidence of our decisions being successful? Have we made the right tradeoffs for the system and our business?

- What is our capability for handling and maintaining tabs on the exposure of information?

- Are we optimizing our capability of information exposure? Is our performance getting better?

- Are we stuck in a specified position? If yes, then is our performance in information exposure declining? What should be done to improve performance?

7: Dimension Two—Threat Intelligence and Its Effectiveness

ACTION: Understand how your organization gathers intelligence and uses it effectively.

Developing intelligence regarding the different people or parties that might want to harm your business by cyberattacks to gain access to information or to overload your server can help you prepare for cyberattacks or attempts.

As the leader of your organization, you should be aware of and understand the various threat agents that pose a threat to your organization and the different measures you can take to protect your organization.

1. Based on the number of times your organization has suffered cyberattack attempts or successes, how effective do you think the organization is at understanding threat agents? Explain.

2. Do you think every threat should warrant your attention? Or do you think threats are a common part of everyday business and it would involve too much time to pay attention to each threat? Explain.

3. If your company does not utilize threat intelligence, what do you consider to be the biggest hindrance or objection?

4. How can internal information leakage affect the number of threat agents to your organization?

Take Action in Your Organization

Know the threats to your organization! Fill in the table below to identify your organization's threat agents, their capabilities, etc.

Threat Agent	Threat Agent Capabilities and Context/Setting in which the Party is a Threat	Your Information that is at Risk	Agent's Potential Method of Attack	Possible Cybersecurity Strategies/Tools

8: Dimension Three—Cyber Interface—Designing and Developing Effectively

ACTION: Taking the size of the organization, understanding how to design and develop a framework to guide the organization's cybersecurity protocols.

The third dimension is focused on the design and development of a cybersecurity interface, along with the design and development of the organization. The design of the cybersecurity interface must take into consideration the size of the organization and the amount of data that is stored on its servers. A framework must be created that helps guide the organization's cybersecurity protocols, thereby protecting the organization from external risk factors. The design must be done carefully after analyzing the various threats faced by the organization, thereby giving clear direction to the cybersecurity professionals regarding the level of security that must be implemented.

Once the design has been created, then comes the process of development. Development includes realizing what the design is and analyzing it to ensure that there are no gaps in the entire process. Once the gaps have been determined, the design should be redefined, and adjustments made accordingly.

1. As a manager, what information can you share with cybersecurity professionals regarding the size and design of your organization to help them determine the level of security needed?

2. Design and development involve activities that are part of a business. List the components that make it a comprehensive dimension.

3. Have the right decisions been made regarding the design and development of your business? Explain.

4. Is the design of your organization's cybersecurity effective in thwarting threats? Explain.

5. How has the design affected the performance of your business? Explain.

6. Is the development of your prepared design effective in protecting and securing confidential data? Explain.

9: Dimension Four—Protection and Control Quality of Cybersecurity

ACTION: Understanding how to set quality controls that create higher security for your organization.

The quality of the controls you use for the protection of private and confidential data will prevent cyberthreats from actively affecting the level of your exposed information. The better these security controls, the higher the security of your data, which can be made even more effective by limiting the exposure of information to unauthorized users.

1. What type of *programs* may help educate the organization's employees about the various cyberthreats and how to overcome them, which protocols to follow in case of a breach, and how to prevent the transfer of information to malicious parties?

2. Managers must decide on *metrics to judge the quality of cybersecurity practices*. Also, determine what would be considered satisfactory performance according to your business standards, identify where the system deficiencies lie, then develop a method to analyze the quality and performance of your company's cybersecurity strategy. This should be done for every individual process and control used for the protection of important data and then, if possible, for the collection of protection controls. Quality of the controls used for protection, as well as the resulting level of protection, must be measured directly. This will give you a better understanding of your cybersecurity controls. **Explain how this can be accomplished in your organization.**

You should also try to determine how quickly and promptly the number of invalid identifications are detected and how they are tackled. Along with this, also consider the following questions:

3. Has your organization developed metrics to judge the quality of cybersecurity practices? If so, do you understand the metrics?

4. List specific ways that you educate the staff about metrics to judge the quality of cybersecurity practices?

5. List six ways you can determine whether the cybersecurity protocols that have been implemented meet standards of quality.

   a.

   b.

   c.

   d.

   e.

   f.

6. In the protection and control quality dimension, cybersecurity professionals may be responsible for the following four factors:

   a.

   b.

   c.

   d.

Take Action in Your Organization

Using established metrics answer and explain the following:

7. How often does the database malfunction?

8. How often are internal threats detected in your system?

9. How often is the database out of sync with the number of *authorized* personnel?

10. How often does the database and cybersecurity system detect incorrectly and provide access to unauthorized personnel?

11. Has your cybersecurity recently updated?

10: Dimension Five—Execution and Operations

ACTION: Understand how to implement the plans that have been created during the protection and controls dimension.

The fifth dimension includes the operations and their executions, how effective they are, and how efficient they can be. It has a similar relationship with the other dimensions as the quality controls dimension. The fifth dimension also encompasses the design and development of the systems, so they can be exposed to the appropriate, relevant parties. The execution and operations dimensions help to implement the plans that have been created during the protection and controls dimension. This is the engine that gets the work done in cybersecurity.

1. It's important to ensure that your system is free of *operational errors*. Name some of the problems that operational errors can cause in your organization and why.

2. Finish this statement: When you view the execution of the decisions you have made regarding the operations of your business; the entire system of operation must be

considered _____ and measured by considering it as a performance dimension and looking at the effectiveness of its results.

3. As a leader, you have the responsibility of overseeing that all operations are performing as intended. If the operations are not performing as intended, what must you do?

4. The quality of the protocols and decisions implemented can affect the _____ _____ of your security protocols.

5. Should cybersecurity objectives be determined and specified before or after the execution of operations? Why? Explain.

6. Change is inevitable in cybersecurity operations. Can you think of changes that can benefit your organization now or in the near future? Explain.

7. Are you prepared to lead forward with the changes? Why or why not? Explain.

8. To support cybersecurity operations, the dimension of execution and operations include the following to help implement cybersecurity strategy:

Take Action in Your Organization

9. In your organization, it is imperative that you decide how can you bring the things designed to reality. Write your explanation for how you can bring the design to reality in your organization. (Hint: the how consists of the action plan that ensures your objectives are met.)

11: Dimension Six—Timely Response and Recovery

ACTION: Understand and utilize a strategy that helps your organization regain the position you lost in the event of a successful cyberattack.

The sixth dimension, which is closely linked to executions and operations, applies to instances when cyberattacks are successful, and your competitors gain an advantage, requiring you to utilize a strategy that helps you regain the position you lost because of the cyberattack. The decision on how to respond in a timely manner and start immediate recovery from a successful cyberattack can be difficult because you must respond to both competitors attempts to take over the market share *and* respond to external and internal threats of your system.

1. The effectiveness of executed operations will determine how quickly you can respond to threats and cyberattacks. The timely response and recovery dimension covers the following five processes:

    _____

    _____

    _____

    _____

    _____

2. In your organization, what are factors that allow the system to continue to operate even when a cyberattack is successful? Explain.

3. Why is a quick response time to a cyberattack critical for your organization in the event of a successful cyberattack? Explain.

4. **Take Action in Your Organization**

   The focus on response and recovery should be how effective, efficient, and quickly the cyberattack was handled to prevent severe data loss. How effective, efficient, and quick is the response and recovery in your organization? Explain, based on your experiences with recovery.

12: Dimension Seven—External Environment—Understanding the Risk Factors

ACTION: Understand how to utilize the external environment dimension to guide cybersecurity and setting requirements and constraints for its operational procedures to make sure the protocols are adept at protecting important data.

The external environment dimension helps guide the cybersecurity and setting requirements and constraints for its operational procedures to ascertain that the protocols are exceptionally adept at protecting important data.

1. Who might have enough of a stake in your organization's demise to launch a severe cyberattack on your company? Explain.

2. Who are the external drivers that help strengthen your cybersecurity?

3. Managing technological relationships is *only part* of the external environment dimension. You must also focus on *how* these relationships can pose a threat to your business or benefit your business. Have you considered whether any of the key players in your external environment can have a direct or indirect harmful influence on your company? Explain.

4. Explain some of the change drivers that may drive change in your organization.

5. Are the procedures and protocols installed in your system in line with industry standards? Explain.

6. Have you considered the various digital platforms that can be used as the basis of attack by any malicious party in the external environment? Explain.

7. Have you considered the changing trends in technology and software, and how they can affect other risk drivers for your organization? Explain.

13: Dimension Eight—Agility and Learning—Innovating Cybersecurity

ACTION: Understand the implementation of cybersecurity and how to restructure and re-engineer it so that it becomes an innovative, new infrastructure that is current.

Utilizing current cybersecurity methods, technology, and software can lower the risk for a successful cyberattack on your organization. Falling behind in cybersecurity and failing to set metrics for improvement can be disastrous for your organization. Even though each individual dimension calls for specific metrics, the whole is not always equal to the sum of its parts. You can't get a clear picture of the loopholes that are present in your cybersecurity system until you have assessed how well the entire system works and considered the effectiveness of each dimension and how well they are interrelated.

1. What does analyzing your entire system's cybersecurity reveal to you? Explain.

2. Using your organization's portfolio of cybersecurity protocols, how well does your organization's entire system work? Explain.

3. What is the worst-case scenario for your system in the near future? Explain.

4. If you go back to the initiating point of cybersecurity in your organization, what assumptions can you challenge that will help improve protocols? Explain.

5. Your security framework must be based on changes happening and be different from the widely-accepted industry standards. Industry standard security protocols that everyone uses makes your organization vulnerable to cyberattacks. What innovative implementations can you and your cybersecurity team insert to help reduce risk in your organization? Explain.

6. As a leader, what have you done or what can you do to prepare your organization for sudden changes in the cybersecurity world?

7. What cybersecurity mistakes have you made in the past that you learned from and will not repeat in the future? Explain.

14: Dimension Nine—Optimizing the Costs Associated with Risks

ACTION: Understand the procedures and processes that help to assess and manage cybersecurity costs.

Dimension nine includes all the procedures and processes that help in the assessment and management of cybersecurity, particularly regarding resources, liabilities, risk mitigation, and forming a balance between the cyber risks faced by an organization and its strengths.

This dimension is concerned with the costs that are associated with cybersecurity, the implementation, failure to comply with the procedures, and ineffective provision of security to the entire framework. All risk factors must be considered financially, and their impact on the financial standing and performance of the company should be considered.

1. As the leader of your organization, do you measure the cost of cybersecurity breaches in your organization every quarter? Explain why or why not.

2. Have you detected a pattern over a few quarters that is helpful for determining what external threats may hit again and the cost to your organization?

3. Make a list of all the risks that might affect your organization and could occur because of activity or incidents related to cybersecurity. Be specific.

15: Dimension Ten—Responsibility and Accountability

ACTION: Understand the importance, responsibility, and accountability for strong cybersecurity in your organization.

The responsibility and accountability dimension deals with the leader's responsibility and accountability to stakeholders and ties all the other dimensions together. All business departments, no matter how large or small, must work together toward clear company objectives for strong cybersecurity throughout the organization.

1. As the leader of your organization, have you requested the cooperation necessary from all departments for implementing strong cybersecurity protocols?

2. Does every department understand their participation and responsibilities for cybersecurity?

3. Besides upper management, who else may make decisions regarding cybersecurity in your organization?

4. In evaluating the way people in your organization take charge of cybersecurity responsibilities, answer these questions for specific departments and individuals:

- How loyal is the employee to the company?

- Is the employee happy with the culture?

- Are they happy with the environment?

- Do they agree with and heed the rules and regulations?

- Do they seem generally dissatisfied?

- How do they react to specific situations?

- Are they good communicators?

- Are they motivated or disengaged?

The answers to the questions above may speak volumes about selecting employees that can successfully handle the responsibility of cybersecurity issues.

16: How to Address Security Threats

ACTION: Understand how to set up, schedule, and initiate tasks that can help protect your network and systems and prevent cyberattacks.

1. List at least five simple ways you can address security threats in your organization and how it helps prevent cyberattacks.

2. Explain how you can implement each task or how you already have implemented each task.

3. You can schedule some tasks to run on computers and mobile devices without any further requirements from you, but other tasks must be initiated by the user. Are your employees properly trained for carrying out these simple tasks? Explain.

4. How often are computers updated in your organization?

5. To avoid passwords that are easy to hack, what are the criteria for password creation in your organization? Explain.

6. Is current software used in your organization? Explain.

7. How often is software evaluated and changed? Explain.

8. Does your organization invest in a reputable cybersecurity expert to check your systems on a regular basis?

17: Cybersecurity for Mobile Devices

ACTIVE: Understand how you can protect your personal and organization's mobile devices from cyberattacks.

Cell phone and mobile device cyberattacks are rampant. Cybercriminals understand that cell phones, tablets, and other mobile devices are used for business in the same ways that laptop or desktop computers are used for business. This makes them targets for cyberattacks.

1. Do you or your staff make the mistake of thinking that cybersecurity is much more important for computers than for cell phones and tablets that you carry around with you? Explain.

2. Why are mobile devices often more vulnerable to cyberattacks than computers that are used only at the office?

3. There are many ways to protect the mobile devices that you and your staff use for business. How proactive are you and your staff with protecting company devices by installing antivirus on your mobile devices that are used for business? Explain.

4. List some of the types of cyberattacks that are common for mobile devices.

5. What should you do if your company mobile device is stolen or you lose it?

6. List 12 ways that you can help protect your mobile devices from falling into the wrong hands or from a cyberattack. Expound on each point.

18: Common Cybersecurity Mistakes

ACTION: Learn everything you can learn about cybersecurity to protect your organization. Hire the best professionals and take advantage of their expertise.

As with everything else in business, the business manager will learn more about cybersecurity as they go. The important thing is to learn as quickly as you can to avoid costly and time-consuming mistakes. Your IT department or professional can be very helpful in sharing their knowledge and expertise with you.

1. Do you believe you can obtain 100% cybersecurity? Why or why not? Explain.

2. Do you believe the most expensive technology automatically provides the best cybersecurity? Why or why not?

3. Do you believe you can win the cyberwar against cybercriminals or it's more effective to create and implement a solid cybersecurity system and do your best to protect against the cybercriminals? Explain.

4. Do you believe the best professionals can prevent all cyberattacks at all times? Why or why not?

About the Author
Mr. Derek Smith, CISSP, MBA, MS, Speaker, Author, and Educator

Derek A. Smith is the founder of the National Cybersecurity Education Center and is responsible for the development and coordination of cybersecurity initiatives at the Center. Formerly he was the Director of Cybersecurity Initiatives at the National Cybersecurity Institute at Excelsior College. Derek has worked for the federal government as a federal agent, cybersecurity manager, and IT program manager. He has also worked for several IT companies including Computer Sciences Corporation and Booz Allen Hamilton.

Derek regularly appears on various news programs as a cybersecurity expert and conducts regular webinars, podcasts, and blogs, and public talks.

Derek is an associate professor at the University of Maryland, University College, Virginia University of Science and Technology and Excelsior College and has taught business and cyber classes for over 25 years. He is also a Board advisor for several boards.

Derek served in the US Navy, Air Force, and Army for a total of 24 years. He has completed an MBA, MS in Digital Forensics, MS in IT Information Assurance, Masters in IT Project Management, and a B.S in Education. Derek also completed all but the dissertation for a Doctorate of Education degree in Organizational Leadership and Conflict and Dispute Resolution.

For fun, Derek has practiced martial arts for over 35 years and hold black belts in several martial arts. He also has acted in movies, television, industrial films, and commercials. Derek is available for consulting, training, and speaking engagements. You can contact him at the National Cybersecurity Education Center at derek@ncseconline.com

Derek lives with his family in Bowie, Maryland. More information about Derek is available at www.Derekamith.com.

www.ingramcontent.com/pod-product-compliance
Lightning Source LLC
LaVergne TN
LVHW082126070326
832902LV00041B/3129